Scottish Surnames

David Dorward

DAVID DORWARD is a graduate in Arts and Law of the University of St Andrews. He practised as a solicitor before joining the staff of his old university, where he enjoys being an administrator among scholars and occasionally aspires to being a scholar among administrators.

Married, with two sons, he engages in the recreations of golf, gardening and fishing, all of which activities combine happily with his favourite hobby of pondering the meanings of names—personal and of place. He is the author of *Scotland's Place-Names*.

Cover illustration by John Mackay

By the same author

SCOTLAND'S PLACE-NAMES

SCOTTISH SURNAMES

David Dorward

Illustrated by John Mackay

WILLIAM BLACKWOOD

First published in 1978 by
William Blackwood & Sons Ltd
32 Thistle Street
Edinburgh EH2 1HA
Scotland

Reprinted 1979

ISBN 0 85158 126 9

Printed at the Press of
the Publisher

"*Must* a name mean something?" Alice asked doubt-fully.

"Of course it must," Humpty Dumpty said with a short laugh: "*my* name means the shape I am—and a good handsome shape it is, too."

Through the Looking-Glass

Contents

Introduction

Spend half a day with the Edinburgh and Glasgow telephone directories and you will have learned quite a bit about Scottish onomatology; spend half a lifetime on and off reading and thinking about these sonorous and evocative names and you will have a considerable appreciation of Scotland, its people and its history.

There is a meaning to every name, and a history behind every surname. The forebears of all of us, Scots and non-Scots, acquired their and our family names in one of four ways: by taking the father's Christian name and using it as a patronymic (e.g. Thomson, MacDonald); by taking the name of one's occupation (e.g. Smith, or its Gaelic equivalent of Gow); by taking a locality name (Fyfe, Sutherland, Wood, Hill, etc.); or by receiving a nickname which sticks (e.g. Brown, Little—or its opposite, Laing). There is a fifth way, which does not create a surname but adopts an existing one, and the classic case is that of the West Indian who called himself MacFarlane out of admiration for the motif on a biscuit tin.

The names which comprise this little book are those which are familiar in Scotland, but not all the commonest Scottish names have been included. What, for example, can one say about Smith, except that it testifies to the importance of the smiter's function; or of Brown, the second commonest name in Scotland, except to wonder how brown was ever a sufficiently distinctive characteristic of anyone to be worth perpetuating? Some of the names are native to Scotland, others came in with immigrants, whether in the twelfth or the nineteenth century. Some are included because they had famous bearers—but remember that no one family is more ancient than any other. Some are included because they illustrate curious features of history or onomatology. All, it is hoped, are of interest to those who love things Scottish and want to know more.

A

ADAM This must surely be the oldest name of them all. As a Christian name it attained great popularity in the twelfth century, particularly in Scotland, but does not emerge as a surname until the reign of James I. Robert Adam (1728-92), the great architect, is the most famous bearer of this form of the name.

Adams is the twenty-sixth commonest name in the U.S.A., but strangely enough this form of the name is not often found in Scotland. Adamson is usual enough here, and is thought to have been particularly popular in Angus, but the characteristic Scottish surname of this genre is formed from the diminutives Adie and Eadie (both surnames in their own right) through Adie-kin, which becomes Aitken. Aitken is therefore a double diminutive, and is our equivalent of the English 'Tommy Atkins'. Soften the 'd' of Adie, add a suffix, and one gets yet another Adam-derivative—Aitchison, which the Americans prefer as Acheson.

The form MacAdam appears in Ayrshire in the sixteenth century; it was the Ayrshire roadbuilder, John Loudon McAdam, whose name was adapted to create the ubiquitous modern term 'tarmac'.

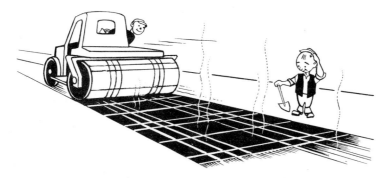

ALEXANDER This Greek name, meaning defender of man, became thoroughly naturalised in Scotland after Queen Margaret, wife of Malcolm Canmore, gave it popularity by

1

bestowing it on her son. There were three Alexander kings of Scotland, and the name has been a firm favourite ever since; in its pet form of Sandy it has become almost synonymous with a Scotsman. As a surname Alexander is no less popular, especially in the west of Scotland.

The Gaelic form is Alastair, which gives the surname MacAlister. The clan MacAlister possessed lands in Kintyre in the fifteenth century, later spreading to Bute and Arran, and on the mainland to Tarbert and Glenbarr. A branch of the clan is said to have settled in Clackmannanshire and Anglicised their name back to Alexander. A Highland origin is therefore possible for the Lowland version of the name, as is so often the case.

ALLAN   The name, with its variants Alan, Allen, etc., has two possible origins: it comes either from the ancient Celtic forename Ailin (*ail* meant a rock in Old Gaelic), and is cognate with Alwyn; or it comes from the Norman name Alan, with its roots in the tribal name Alemannus, which is approximately what the French call the Germans in politer moments. The name Alan became popular in Scotland through its adoption as a forename by the Stewarts, and even before then Sir Alan Durward was a noted figure in the Scotland of Robert I.

ANDERSON   The cult of St Andrew was introduced to Scotland in the early Middle Ages, and became a focus for nationalism in the twelfth and thirteenth centuries. Andrew consequently became a very popular Christian name in this country (it is now *the* most popular), and its derivative Anderson is the ninth commonest Scottish surname. The earlier form of the name was Androsoun, later Andrewson, but by the fifteenth century was metathesised into its modern form.

MacAndrew is the Highland form of the name and in this context probably means son of the servant of St Andrew; this is made explicit in the other Gaelic form of the name, Gillanders (see GILCHRIST).

2

Andrews (which also means son of Andrew) is not native to Scotland, but is found mainly in southern England.

B

BARCLAY Spelling is not normally very important in the study of surnames, because orthography was not standardised until the nineteenth century and even later. But spelling is all that differentiates Barclay from the English place-name Berkeley ('birch lea'), from which it derives. The name is found in Scotland as early as 1165.

A Scottish Barclay made his fortune in the Thirty Years War and acquired the estate of Urie near Stonehaven in the seventeenth century. Another branch of the family, the Towie-Barclays, produced the famous soldier Prince Barclay de Tolly who commanded the Russian army which defeated Napoleon in 1812.

The name belongs mainly to the north-east of Scotland, although a branch was established in Ayrshire.

BELL The most likely derivation of this name is the Old French *le bel*, meaning the handsome man. There must have been no shortage of bonnie lads in medieval Scotland, because Bell is now the thirty-fourth commonest surname here. (It is worth noting that complimentary nicknames tend to be perpetuated as surnames more than do slighting ones: Sharp and

3

Smart mean exactly what they say, while there are no surnames signifying the stupidity of the bearer.)

Another possible derivation is a locality one—from habi-
tation near the town bell—or even an occupational one of
bell-ringer. The derivation 'son of Isobel' is unlikely: offspring very seldom took their surname from the maternal
Christian name, because to do so would imply that the
father was unknown. There are a few English surnames of
this type, such as Ibbs and Tillett (son of Isobel and
Matilda respectively). But who has heard of an Elizabeth-
son or a MacMargaret?

BOYLE   This name would only just scrape into the list of
the hundred commonest Scottish surnames. It has two
totally different origins. One is from the village of Boyville,
near Caen, and in 1291 the Norman Henry de Boyville is
recorded as castellan of the castles of Dumfries, Wigtown
and Kirkcudbright. The name is still fairly common in these
districts, where it was pronounced 'Bole'.

The other derivation is from the ancient Irish forename
Baoghail, which apparently has the complicated meaning of
'having profitable pledges'. It is likely that most Scottish
Boyles are of Irish stock, for the name is among the fifty
commonest in Ireland. Boyle is the family name of the earls
of Cork and Orrery, Glasgow and Shannon.

Boyd is quite different: it means 'of Bute'.

BRUCE   The Bruces were not, as is sometimes said,
Anglo-Norman opportunists who threw in their lot with the
Scots when they saw a crown within their grasp. The Bruce
family had been established in Annandale for five generations prior to Bannockburn, and the circumstance of their
also holding lands in England made them no different from
any other noble of the time; indeed, David I, King of Scots,
was an English Baron before his succession to the throne in
1164.

The family name is certainly Norman, deriving from the
lands of Brus (now Brix), near Cherbourg, whence came also

4

the Stewarts and the Cunninghams. The first Robert de Brus crossed the Channel with William the Conqueror, the second Robert Bruce accompanied David I to claim his Scottish throne. Six generations later this 'Norman' family produced the man who was to make himself the ruler of an independent Kingdom of Scotland.

The royal Bruce line died out just over fifty years after Bannockburn, but offshoots of the family were granted lands in Clackmannan and Fife. To one of them was given the Lordship of Kinloss, and later the earldom of Elgin, and this is the senior branch of the Bruce family today.

BUCHANAN There is a district of Buchanan on the eastern shores of Loch Lomond, whence the clan gets its appellation. The place-name comes from the Gaelic *both chanain*, meaning Canon's bothy or house. (*Both* on its own gives the surname Boath.)

The original name of the inhabitants of this district was MacAuslan (son of Absalom), and one Gilbride MacAuslan, a major-domo of the Earl of Arran, acquired lands in Buchanan and subsequently took a new surname from them. Although the chiefship died out in 1682, there were numerous branches of the clan which flourished in the district for many years afterwards. James Buchanan (1791-1868), fifteenth President of the United States, commemorated his native heath by giving his name to a county in Missouri.

The name has no connection with Buchan, which is a district in Aberdeenshire.

BURNS Like many another famous Scot, the poet Robert Burns had a name that was thoroughly English in linguistic origin. The word 'burn', used universally in Scotland to mean any watercourse from a tiny streamlet to a young river, is pure Anglo-Saxon. The poet's father's name was in fact Burness (still found in that form in Kincardineshire, where the family came from) and represents the genitive case of the word. The name therefore means 'of the burns'—that is, living by the waters.

Burns is a fairly common name in Scotland, but not because of the fecundity of the poet. Ours is a well-watered country, and many a family must have taken its surname from the fact of living by a burn. Other Scottish names of similar origin are Muir and Moore (on the moor), Green, Knox (at the knock or hill) and Hyslop (at the hazel hope or valley).

C

CAMERON   It used to be believed that the name Cameron comes from the Gaelic words *cam sron* meaning crooked nose, and indeed a Miss Cameron recently said of a Miss Campbell that she would rather have a squint nose than a wry mouth (see following). But the earliest form of the name is Cambron, and the persistence of the mediant 'b' in the written records has led modern scholars to the belief that the name comes from the lands of Camberone (now Cameron parish) in Fife. It is certainly true that one famous bearer of the name, Richard Cameron, was a Fifer and a fanatical Covenanter; the Cameronian regiment was raised in his honour.

Whatever the origin of their name, the Camerons were one of the most ancient and warlike of the Highland clans. By the fourteenth century the clan had become established in Lochaber, which is still very much Cameron country. They were among the staunchest supporters of the House of Stewart, and the '45 would probably have fizzled out at Glenfinnan had not Lochiel appeared on the scene with his 700 Cameron clansmen.

Although the clan was numerous and powerful, the surname Cameron is not nearly so common as, say, MacDonald or Stewart, the reason being that not all of the clan actually bore the clan surname. Many of them rejoiced in the ancient patronymics of MacChlerich, MacGillonie, MacIldowie, MacOnie, MacOurlie, MacWalrick, MacEantach and MacAngus, which they shed for something more manageable when they left their native glens.

CAMPBELL The name comes from two Gaelic words, *cam* meaning crooked and *beul* meaning mouth, and it is not often that an uncomplimentary nickname attains the dignity of a surname. (Forget the attempted derivation *de Campo Bello*—Latin was not much spoken in Campbell country.)

Who the original Crooked Mouth was we shall never know, for the clan has its legendary origin in the mists of Ossianic saga, and its earliest known history is in the ancient Scottish kingdom of Dalriada, now Lorne and Argyll.

The Campbells were either far-sighted or fortunate in their alliances. Rewarded for their support of Robert the Bruce, they used their increasing power to oppose the MacDonald Lordship of the Isles; they later contrived to be on the winning side in the Civil Wars and Jacobite rebellions, and consequently suffered less than other clans from the destruction of clan power in the mid-eighteenth century. By Victoria's reign there were no less than forty Campbell estates in Scotland, amounting to almost 1,250,000 acres of land. Most of it was owned by the Duke of Argyll, but there were large acreages in Perthshire, Stirlingshire, Ayrshire and at Cawdor in Nairnshire.

The Campbells were a very numerous clan, and an unusually large number of the clansmen actually bore the clan surname; when, during the aftermath of the '45, a Stewart was being tried for the Appin murder, no less than eleven of the jury of fifteen (empanelled presumably at random) were named Campbell. There is also, of course, the fact that in the seventeenth and eighteenth centuries it paid to assume the name Campbell (see MacGREGOR).

CHRISTIE   Christian (meaning what it says) was a common forename in the Middle Ages, and its diminutive form gives the surname Christie, which appears to have had its origin in Fife, where it is still common. Christison is also found, and the form MacChristie has been recorded in Galloway.

   Oddly enough, the form Christopher ('Christ-bearing') never had much vogue in Scotland except in the diminutive form Christo and Chrystal; the second of these was used both as a Christian name (for boys and girls alike) and as a surname.

CLARK   In the early Middle Ages almost everyone who could write was entitled to style himself *clericus*, and the word appears after many a signature in documents of pre-surname days. When Latin ceased to be universally used in documents the word appears as Le Clerc and it is not always possible to determine when it becomes a surname rather than a description. However, the standard of literacy in Scotland must have been reasonably high, or else clerks were particularly prolific, because by the fifteenth century the name was spread throughout the land and today it is the thirteenth commonest Scottish surname. It is also common in England, sometimes in the form Clarke.

   The term clerk (which meant secretary, scribe, scholar or cleric) passed into Gaelic, giving the designation *Mac a chleirich* which survives only in its Irish form McCleary and in its translated form Clarkson.

CRAIG   The Welsh word for rock is *craig*, and the Gaelic word is *creag*, both passing into English as crag. The surname Craig was applied to a dweller near the crag, and it is the Welsh spelling which has survived in the surname—

note, however, that the Picts are thought to have spoken a form of Celtic akin to Welsh, and many topographical features in Scotland have Welsh-type name-elements, such as *aber* (estuary), *caer* (fort) and *tref* (homestead).

The name Craig appears to have originated from many different localities, and there are one or two compounds such as Craigmyle and Craigie which are place-names that have given rise to surnames.

Craik is a different name, taken by a family who came from the village of Crayke in Yorkshire in the fifteenth century.

CRAWFORD   There is a barony of Crawford in rural Lanarkshire, and it means 'ford of the crows'. As a surname, Crawford appears in many charters from the twelfth century onwards. A daughter of Sir John of Crawford married David Lindsay, ancestor of the Earls of Crawford; her sister married Sir Malcolm Wallace and in due course became the mother of the first great Scottish patriot.

The Crawfords were never a clan but a Lowland family of great distinction; the branches of Auchinames, Craufurdland and Kilbirnie are the most notable.

CUNNINGHAM   This is the name of a district in Ayrshire, and the curiously southern 'ham' ending is the work of an anglophile scribe. The original form of the place-name was Cunegan, but the meaning has never been satisfactorily explained.

A Norman adventurer was given the manor of Cunningham in Ayrshire in the twelfth century, and following common practice adopted a surname from his property. The family acquired by marriage the lands of Glencairn, and by the fifteenth century they had been raised to the peerage. It was the 14th earl of Glencairn who was the friend and patron of Robert Burns; the poet named his fourth (legitimate) son James Glencairn Burns.

The Cunninghams (they were never a clan) are recorded in various parts of Scotland from the fifteenth century onwards. A family of Cunninghams from Ayrshire migrated to Strathblane in the sixteenth century and the name turns up soon afterwards in Fife and Edinburgh. It is even said to have emigrated to France in the form Conigans.

D

DAVIDSON   David was a royal name in Scotland as well as in Judea (it is a Hebrew word meaning beloved), and there were many Scots who took the patronymic Davidson. Although mainly a Lowland surname, there was a Highland clan of Davidsons in Badenoch, so given to sanguinary feuding that they became virtually extinct in the Middle Ages. Legend, if not history, has it that at the famous Battle of the Clans on the North Inch in Perth in 1396 the Davidsons were one of the two contesting clans, and that the whole contingent were exterminated save one.

The Lowland Davidsons were more peaceable, being douce burgesses in Aberdeen and Dundee, as the records show. The diminutive form of the name, Davie, is recorded frequently, but very seldom Davies—one has to go to Wales to find *them*. Another diminutive of David was Daw, which gives Dawson.

DICKSON   Richard, of which Dick is one of the many diminutives, is a Germanic forename popularised in this country by the Normans. The first syllable means powerful, the second brave. Richardson and Dickson are common in Scotland; Richards and Dixon tend to be English forms.

Of the diminutive forms, Scotland has Dick, Dickie and Dickson as surnames. Of the English type of diminutives, Dickens, Dickinson, there is no trace in Scotland. Rhyming diminutives like Hick never caught on here either, and we have no native Hickses, Hickeys or Higginses.

The most characteristic Scottish name from this source is Ritchie, which started life as the Christian name Richie. Ritchie, like Dickson, was originally a Border surname but is now fairly widespread.

10

DOUGLAS   This is a place-name which became a famous surname and now has perhaps its widest currency as a male Christian name. It is in fact a river name from the Gaelic *dubh glais* meaning black water, a descriptive term which occurs frequently in Scottish topography. Douglas was unknown as a Christian name until the sixteenth century, and even then as often as not it was a girl's name.

The first member of the family to be recorded in Scotland is William de Douglas in the twelfth century, and there were four main branches of the family in medieval times: (1) the Black Douglases of Douglasdale, the most famous of whom was the Sir James Douglas who attempted to take the Bruce's heart to the Holy Land for burial; (2) the Douglas Earls of Morton in Dumfriesshire; (3) the Red Douglas Earls of Angus; and (4) the Drumlanrig branch who became Marquesses of Queensberry. 'None durst strive against a Douglas' was the sixteenth-century saying when the family was at the height of its power; and indeed the history of medieval Scotland is inseparably bound up with the rise and fall of the various branches of the house of Douglas.

DRUMMOND   The Gaelic word for back, or spine or ridge is *druim*, plural *dromannan*, and this gives several place-names, including Drymen in Stirlingshire. Malcolm Beg, so called from his small size, married a daughter of the Earl of Lennox, and his descendants took their surname from the lands of Drymen. The family acquired by marriage the estates of Stobhall and Cargill, and the clan's centre of gravity moved to eastern Perthshire, where it remains still. Numerous cadet branches have occupied lands ranging from Glenartney in the west, through the lovely valley of Strathearn to the fringes of the city of Perth. Drummonds are still fairly thick on the ground in that part of Perthshire.

The Drummonds were always arch-royalists, supporters in turn of Robert the Bruce, Mary, Queen of Scots, the great Montrose, and the Old and Young Chevaliers. The chief became Earl of Perth, and the title was elevated into a short-lived Jacobite dukedom. Lord John Drummond held the rank of Lieutenant-General in the Jacobite army in 1745. The Drummond lands were forfeited thereafter but restored in 1784; and a Drummond, Earl of Perth, still lives in the ancient mansion of Stobhall.

DUNCAN This is a version of the Celtic personal name Donnchad, which is commonly taken to come from the

Gaelic *donn cath* meaning brown warrior—doubtful, however, because the adjective normally follows the noun in that language. Duncan was never a clan name, but became a common surname all over the Lowlands and as far south as Berwick. The form Duncanson is also found.

A Duncan who lived in Atholl in pre-surname days, nicknamed 'the Fat' (*Donnchadh Reamhar*), had a grandson Robert who was progenitor of the clan Robertson (q.v.). But the clan is properly known as Clan Donnchaidh or Donnachie (the 'children of Duncan'), and the surnames Duncan, Donnachie and MacConachie are still commonly found in Perthshire.

E

ELLIOT There are no fewer than seventy different ways of spelling this celebrated Border surname, ranging from

'Allat' to 'Ellwood'; it probably derives from Old English Aelfwald ('elf-ruler') which became the Christian name Elwald. It was a particularly common forename in the Borders, but seems almost to have dropped out of use as such when it became a surname in the fifteenth century.

Although it is not strictly correct to speak of a Border 'clan' (a concept which belongs to the Gaelic-speaking Highlands), the old Border families such as the Elliots and the Armstrongs lived by the sword in a manner reminiscent of the Highlanders. Hired by the central government to protect the Scottish Border, they lost their usefulness after the Union of the Crowns and were subjected to 'clearances' no less cruel that those in the north two centuries later.

The senior branch of the Elliot 'clan' was that of Stobs, which was raised to a baronetcy in the eighteenth century. Another branch became baronets of Minto, and it was Jane Elliot of this line who wrote 'The Flowers of the Forest'.

F

FARQUHAR Farquhar comes from the Old Gaelic *fearchar* and means dear one. It was a popular Celtic forename, and is recorded (in some very bizarre spellings) virtually all over medieval Scotland.

As a surname it is perhaps commoner in the form Farquharson. A fourteenth-century warrior named Fearchar

Shaw, himself related to the MacIntosh chiefs, founded a dynasty who took the name Farquharson. Their progeny flourished on the braes of Angus and Mar where the name is still found. Particularly notable are the Farquharsons of Invercauld and formerly of Balmoral, which latter property they sold to Queen Victoria.

When combined with the Mac prefix, Farquhar becomes McKerchar, which is a Perthshire name. The contraction Kerracher is also found.

FERGUSSON The original Scots were a Gaelic-speaking people who began infiltrating the south-west Highlands from Ireland about the year 500, and the first recorded settlement was made by one Fergus Mor. Fergus Mor has, with more enthusiasm than accuracy, been hailed as the founder of Scotland's monarchy, but there is no clan Fergusson derived from him. What happened in effect was that the personal name Fergus (it means 'super-choice') acquired great prestige and popularity in both Scotland and Ireland, and many families of completely different origin took the surname Fergusson. Perhaps the best-known family is that of Ayrshire, whose ancestors were awarded the lands of Kilkerran by King Robert the Bruce.

The Highland sons of Fergus were known as 'Mac-Fhearghas': the 'Fh' being silent the name was transliterated as MacKerras.

FLEMING Among the most welcome incomers to Scotland in the early Middle Ages, because of the stimulus to the wool trade, were the men from Flanders—the Flemings. The Flemish traders for their part were particularly glad to come to Scotland, because in 1155 Henry II of England had expelled them from his country.

Not all Flemish immigrants took the name Fleming. One family, for example, obtained the lands of Innes in Aberdeenshire and took their surname from the property.

Another Flemish family acquired the lands of Douglas Water, and again took a native surname from their territories (see DOUGLAS). Yet another settled in Fife and took the name Young (q.v.).

Very many of them, however, must have taken a surname from their country of origin, for Fleming is today among the hundred commonest names here.

FLETCHER A *fléchier* in Old French was an arrow-maker, and as an occupational name Fletcher was known throughout Britain. The trade was as common in the High-lands as elsewhere, and the Gaelic word is *fleisdear*, giving the surname *Mac an Fhleistear* which was in turn anglicised to Fletcher. The Fletchers of Glenlyon were hereditary sup-pliers of arrows to the MacGregors.

There is, however, a completely different trade which can give rise to the surname, and that is flesher (the common name for butcher in Scotland). Butchering must have been a very important occupation, and the other surname that comes from it, Butcher, is very uncommon. (Butchart is from the French *bouchard*, meaning bottle-corker.) In the Scottish records of the seventeenth century the two words Fletcher and Flesher became hopelessly confused.

A Fletcher therefore cannot tell by linguistic evidence alone whether his ancestors were arrowsmiths or butchers, or Gaelic- or English-speakers.

FORBES There is a distressing modern tendency to pro-nounce this name as 'Fawbs'. The correct bi-syllabic render-ing is illustrated by the circumstances of one Tom Forbes who enlisted in the French army and had his name registered as 'Fort Bays'.

The name comes from the lands of Forbes in Aberdeenshire, and it preserves the Brythonic place-name element *fothair*, meaning wood or copse, which usually passed into Gaelic as *for* or *fetter* (Fordun, Fordyce, Fettercairn). (Forsyth is different, however, being derived from the Celtic personal name *fear-sith*, meaning man of peace; it should be pronounced with the stress on the second syllable.)

Forbes was and is the name of a well-known Aberdeenshire clan, who had held lands in Strathdon long before they were erected into a barony in 1271. Alexander Forbes was raised to the peerage by James I, and his descendants formed other dynastic branches of the clan in various parts of the north-east, including Pitsligo, Culloden, Craigievar and Monymusk. As Protestants the Forbes clan were in continual rivalry with their all-powerful Gordon neighbours.

FRASER There is a temptation to conceive of the typical Highland clan as being of very ancient and mythic origin, with lands which have been in the common possession of the tribe since prehistory, defended at sword point against all comers. But in fact many of the most celebrated of Highland clans have a totally different origin. The early Scottish kings would grant land to Norman or Flemish adventurers from the south; and in the reign of Malcolm IV the policy of replacing turbulent and disaffected Celtic chiefs with followers who spoke the English language became endemic. By the end of the twelfth century almost the whole of cultivable Scotland was held by feudal magnates, who were obliged to perform certain duties (including military service) for the sovereign. In time each landowner would grant leases to his near relations, who would continue the process with their own descendants, until with intermarriage something approaching a dynastic kindred was established.

Such is the history of the clan Fraser. A Norman knight named Frizel brought the name to Scotland: his descendants played a heroic part in the fourteenth-century Wars of Independence and were awarded lands in Buchan, becoming the Lords Saltoun, and founding the town of Fraserburgh. A cadet branch of the clan married into properties in Ross-shire, and were raised to the peerage in the person of the 1st Lord Lovat. In time the Frasers became a genuine Gaelic-speaking Highland clan (as their neighbours the Gordons did not), and to this day Fraser is one of the commonest names in the Inverness area. It was probably even commoner in the eighteenth century, when the clan was able to muster a body of 600 men at Culloden; and, being resident in the vicinity, the luckless Frasers bore the brunt of the subsequent reprisals.

G

GIBSON Gilbert is one of these double-barrelled Germanic forenames, totemistic in character and with no intelligible meaning as it stands; its constituent parts mean 'hostage' and 'bright', which were both 'in words' in a society which was always on a war footing. Gilbert, like many such names, was introduced to England by the Normans, and became popular as a Christian name in Scotland. It was the name of Robert Burns's younger brother; and was frequently contracted to Gib.

As surnames, Gibbs and Gibbon are frequently found in England; but the characteristic Scottish surname from Gilbert is Gibson and it cannot be placed in any particular Lowland locality. The form MacGibbon appears sporadically in Highland records; MacGilbert, although recorded, appears now to be extinct.

GILCHRIST The early Highlanders were fond of religious appellations, and often named their children in a dedicatory fashion. The word used to express this idea is *gille*, which means servant or lad. Gilchrist is therefore 'a follower or servant of Christ', and there are quite a number of these Gil- names in Scotland. Most often the dedication is to a particular saint, of which Gaeldom had a vast number, e.g. Gilbride (St Bridget), Gilfeather (St Peter), Guilfoyle (St Paul), Gillanders (St Andrew), Gilfillan (St Fillan), Gillan and Gilzean (St John), and Gilmartin (St Martin). The Gaelic word for Jesus is *Iosa*, giving the name Gillies, while *Moire* is the Virgin Mary, giving us Gilmour. Gillespie means the bishop's servant. Gilroy and Gilruth have no religious connection but are anglicisations of *gille ruadh*—the red-headed lad.

GORDON Sir Adam of Gordon (a place in Berwickshire) was rewarded by Robert the Bruce with the lordship of Strathbogie in Aberdeenshire, and the family acquired additional estates in the wake of the departed Comyns, becoming

lords of Badenoch. The weakness of central government in the early Middle Ages made it important for the Crown to have strong men in the regions, and what the Campbells were to the south-west Highlands the Gordons were to the north-east. An earldom (of Huntly) followed by a marquessate and finally a dukedom were the rewards of this family's not always disinterested service. Another branch of the family (one should not call it a clan), the Gordons of Haddo, became Earls of Aberdeen.

The Gordons are of interest as being a family rather than a tribal clan. Although all-powerful in the north it was as landowners and not as patriarchal chiefs that they drew their strength. The lordship of Badenoch made the Gordons the feudal superiors of the inhabitants of the upper Spey valley, but such were the ties of kinship that these thoroughly Celtic clansmen followed their own MacIntosh and MacPherson chiefs in defiance of their legal Gordon overlords, whom they regarded as alien instruments of government.

The 1st Earl of Huntly is supposed to have laid the foundations of his 'clan' by rewarding all who took the name Gordon with a gift of meal; thus certain of his followers were called the 'Bow' o' Meal' Gordons to distinguish them from the true stock.

GRAHAM   This name is of pure Anglo-Saxon origin and comes from *graeg ham* or grey home, an English manor mentioned in Domesday Book. (Legends about Grimm's Dyke are now discounted.) William de Graham accompanied David I to Scotland on his return from England, and the family rose to great prominence in the Wars of Independence.

This is not the place to recount the exploits of the great Montrose or of Claverhouse (both of them Grahams, and staunch supporters of the Royalist cause in the seventeenth century), but mention must be made of James Graham, 3rd Duke of Montrose, who as a Member of Parliament was responsible for legislation in 1782 to repeal the infamous act of 1747 which rendered it a criminal act to wear Highland dress.

The Grahams were not a Highland clan but a Lowland family, with numerous branches in Menteith, Drymen, the Borders and Angus. The romantic but incorrect spelling Graeme appears to have been introduced by the scholar George Buchanan in the sixteenth century.

GRANT   This nickname appears to have started life as Le Grand, and was applied to a Nottinghamshire property-owner who acquired lands in Inverness-shire in the thirteenth century. From these not untypical beginnings the great clan Grant arose, with its base in Strathspey but having

19

branches in Glenmoriston and Aberdeenshire. The Grant lands in Strathspey were elevated into a regality after the Glorious Revolution of 1688, and Sir Ludovic Grant of Freuchie built the model village known today as Grantown-on-Spey. Although the Grant chiefs were anti-Jacobite in sympathy they lost their hereditary jurisdictions with all the others in 1747. Intermarriage with the daughter of the Earl of Seafield brought that title into the family, and there were three other Grant baronetcies.

The Grants are a typical case of a clan which got a foothold in the Highlands through marriage-settlement or other legal means and extended their possessions by the sword. Feudalism reverted to tribalism in a surprisingly short time, and the clan memory took no account of its non-Celtic origin; indeed the Grants firmly believed that they were descended, like the MacGregors, from Alpin, King of Scots.

The likelihood is that most Scottish Grants had their origin in Strathspey as ordinary tenants of their incomer-landlord; although having no real kinship with him, they would take his surname and claim his chiefly protection. Most of them would have not the slightest idea of the latent grandeur of the name.

GRAY Of the bearers of this name Auld Robin Gray is the one that comes most readily to mind, but there are many others, for this is among the thirty commonest Scottish surnames. It is clearly a nickname, presumably from the colour of the hair, or possibly the clothing, and is distributed evenly throughout the Lowlands. It is sometimes claimed that the first bearers of the name came from the town of Gray in Haute-Saône, but the simpler adjectival origin is more likely.

The Gaelic word for grey is *glas*, which gives the surname Glass, common at one time in Perth and Dunblane. The common Gaelic patronymic from the adjective, however, is *mac ghille ghlaisan*—the son of the grey man—which is rendered as MacGlashan and was not infrequently converted into the Lowland form Gray.

20

The other adjectives of colour—brown, black and white—also give common Lowland surnames, and their Gaelic equivalents are respectively *donn* (which gives Dunn), *dubh* (which gives Dow and Duff) and *ban* (which gives Bain). For red, see REID.

GUNN What the MacGregors were to the southern Highlands the Gunns were to the northern: set about by powerful enemies—the earls of Sutherland and Caithness on the one side, the MacKays on the other—the clan Gunn had a continual struggle for survival throughout the Middle Ages. The Highland clearances of the early nineteenth century finally deprived them of their ancient territories, and those members of the clan who did not emigrate were forced to eke out a living in the coastal villages.

Authorities cannot agree on the origins of either the clan or the name. Were the Gunns descendants of the Gunni of the Norse sagas, or does the name come from Norse *gunnr* meaning war or from the Gaelic *guineach* meaning fierce? Or are the Gunns older still, a remnant of the once-powerful race of Picts who retreated from the Gaelic Scots of the south-west and from the Viking raiders? Certainly, the number of Pictish remains in the traditional Gunn country might favour the latter theory, but the truth will probably never be known.

Gunn is not one of the commoner Scottish names, but it is one of immense distinction. Neil M. Gunn, son of a Caithness skipper, was until his death in 1973 the greatest living Scottish novelist—perhaps he is now the greatest of all time. His masterpiece *The Silver Darlings* enshrines all the qualities that made his clan a force in the land.

H

HAMILTON Hambledon means crooked hill and occurs as a place-name in Hampshire, Surrey and Dorset, with the variants Hambleton and Hambleden in other English counties. Whatever his exact place of origin, there was a Walter

Fitz Gilbert de Hameldone who possessed properties in Renfrewshire during the Wars of Independence. For his services to the Bruce he was duly rewarded with the Comyn lands in Lanarkshire, which in turn were named after him— the modern town of Hamilton. As a result of marriage with royalty in 1474 the 2nd Lord Hamilton was created Earl of Arran; the succeeding earl became Marquess of Hamilton, and the 3rd Marquess became the 1st Duke of Hamilton.

There are many Hamiltons in Scotland and elsewhere who would not claim descent from the ducal family or its many aristocratic offshoots. It is likely that these humbler Hamiltons derive their name from the Lanarkshire town rather than from the original 'crooked hill'.

HAY   Having nothing to do with dried grass, this name comes from a place in Normandy called La Haye (which itself derives from *haie* meaning hedge). The first of the name in Scotland was William de Haya who obtained lands in Erroll in the Carse of Gowrie from William the Lion at the end of the twelfth century. The family rose rapidly in importance, becoming Lords of Errol and Lord High Constables of Scotland. Other branches became earls of Kinnoull and Marquesses of Tweeddale. The Clan Hay Society has its headquarters at yet another family seat, Delgatie Castle.

The name is still among the more familiar Scottish surnames, and, since it does not appear to have any other possible linguistic origin, most of the present-day Hays may fairly claim descent from one of the Norman adventurers.

HENDERSON   Henry has long been a popular Christian name, and it occurs in this form as a surname in Scotland, particularly in Ayrshire and Fife. The origin is the Old German *heim reich* meaning 'home ruler' (but not in the sense of separatist). It also appeared in the form Henryson, the name of one of the greatest of our medieval poets; but in Scots the letter 'd' tends to intrude, giving us the names Hendry and Henderson.

The Hendersons were never a clan in the strict sense of the word, but there are three distinct branches of the family. The most notable is Henderson of Fordell in Fife, whose earlier name was Henryson and who came originally from Dumfriesshire. In the far north a chieftain of the clan Gunn had a younger son Henry who founded a family of Hendersons in Caithness; and there was also a Henderson sept of the MacDonalds of Glencoe. The word sept should not be employed indiscriminately. It is strictly a branch of dynastic kindred bearing a different surname from the chief. The Hendersons were of the original Glencoe stock, and when the chiefship passed to an heiress of different name (MacDonald) they retained an honoured place in the life of the clan. Quite different from the broken men who hung about the fringes of most of the large clans and were taken under the chief's protection; these latter should not be called septs, although they very often are. The Glencoe Hendersons were also known by their Gaelic name MacEanruig, whose modern form is McKendrick.

HERD   In country parts of Scotland this word still means the herdsman rather than the flock. In earlier times when hedges were few and fences non-existent the only way to keep the 'bestial' in about and protect them from predators (human and animal) was to employ someone to do it. The herdsman's function was a vital one, and it has given us the surname Herd or Hird.

There were numerous kinds of flock, and each one had its own herdsman. Shepherd is the most familiar, and Coward (cow-herd) is celebrated if uncommon. But there were also herders of calves, giving the name Calvert; of stots (bullocks)

giving us Stoddart; of colts, giving Coltart and Coulthard; of hogs, giving us Hoggart; and of wethers (castrated rams) giving us Weatherhead. Most of these trades are now obsolete, but the surnames preserve for us the memory of a bygone way of Scottish life.

HUGHES   This name is normally thought of as Welsh, with a large English distribution, but nevertheless Hughes is among the hundred commonest Scottish surnames, and the process of English immigration does not account for its high incidence.

Hughes means son of Hugh, which is cognate with Hugo; it derives from the Old German *hugu*, meaning heart or mind. The typical Scottish spelling of Hugh is Hew, and gives the diminutives Hewitt, Howat and Howie, all familiar enough Scottish names although not as common as Hughes.

An old French form of Hugh was Huchon, which was barbarously pronounced as Hutcheon in Scots. This produces the names Hutchinson and Hutcheson, with the Highland form MacCutcheon. MacCutcheon therefore means exactly the same as Hughes; but McHugh is different, being an Irish corruption of 'son of Aodh' (see MacKAY).

JAMESON   Although James was the Christian name of seven Stewart kings (eight by the Jacobite reckoning) and has always been a popular baptismal name, it never seems to have become a surname in its own right in Scotland. It is common enough in England and America (cf. Henry James the novelist). Jameson (pronounced 'Jimmie-son') is the Scottish form, and was common in Bute and the West of Scotland from earliest times. Another spelling is Jamieson.

A Highland form MacJames is recorded, but is very rarely found nowadays. The Gaelic version of James is Seumas (more familiarly, Hamish), but it does not figure as a surname.

JOHNSTON   In medieval times the city of Perth was known as St John's toun or St Johnston, and many of its natives took their name from it. Indeed when the clan Gregor was proscribed some Perth MacGregors are said to have renounced their 'unhappie name' and assumed that of Johnston. There were doubtless other 'touns' or homesteads belonging to someone called John which would give rise to surnames; for example, the Border family of Johnstone took their name from the parish of Johnstone in Dumfriesshire. A completely different family of Johnstones had lands in Strathspey.

Although John was the most popular Christian name in medieval Scotland, the patronymic Johnson is curiously uncommon north of the Border. The Gaelic form of John is Ian, but who has heard of many Iansons? And although MacIan was the chiefly name of the MacDonalds of Glencoe, it never gained wide currency as a surname. A small clan of MacIans in Ardnamurchan were swindled out of their ancestral possessions by the Campbells in the seventeenth century, forced to a life of crime and obliged eventually to relinquish the clan name. Some of them settled in Lochaber and became Johnstones (not Johnsons, which would have been etymologically more correct).

K

KELLY This name is among the fifty commonest in Scotland. But significantly it is also the second commonest Irish surname, and the vast majority of the Scottish Kellys are originally of Irish stock. Not all, however, for there are lands of Kellie in Fife and Angus (the name comes from the Gaelic *coille*, meaning a wood) and some bearers of the name will have originated in these places; for example, a John de Kelly was Abbot of Arbroath in 1373. The Irish version of the name is from O Ceallaigh, meaning 'descendant of war'.

Many Irish surnames are so common in Scotland as to have become naturalised (e.g. Docherty and Gallacher), and others, like Kennedy, reflect the fact that the Scots and the Irish share a common linguistic heritage. Irish immigration began in the late eighteenth century and reached a flood with the potato famine of the 1840s. There has been nothing like it since; the Italian immigration of the early twentieth century was a mere trickle by comparison, and although every Scottish village has its Italian ice-cream or fish restaurant (what would we do without them?) no single Italian surname has become sufficiently common to have become naturalised. Subsequent immigrations will probably leave their mark, although it is unlikely that the names Novak and Patel will ever become as familiar in Scotland as Kelly and Docherty.

KENNEDY The Kennedys were the dominant family in south-west Scotland at a time when that part of the country was Gaelic-speaking. The name itself is thoroughly Celtic, comprising the words *ceann eitigh*, probably meaning 'grim-headed'. When first recorded the name is always prefixed by Mac, which confirms that Kennedy was originally a forename (but unconnected with Kenneth).

The Kennedys of Dunure succeeded to the lands of Carrick, and after a royal marriage were elevated to the peerage as Lords Kennedy. A brother of the 1st Lord Kennedy, James Kennedy, Bishop of St Andrews and Chancellor of the University, was one of the most notable statesmen of medieval Scotland; his college in St Andrews still flourishes. The 3rd Lord Kennedy was created Earl of Cassilis four years before he died at Flodden. The family later built the splendid Castle of Culzean.

26

The family name also made its way to the north-east, where Kennedys are recorded in the Aberdeen annals in the fourteenth century. One Ulric Kennedy went from Carrick to Lochaber in the sixteenth century; his descendants were known by the curious name of MacWalrick and acknowledged the leadership of the Cameron clan among whom they lived.

The Irish Kennedys are of the family O Cinneide, which originated in County Clare. To say that the Scottish Kennedys are by remote origin Irish is to do no more than recall that the entire original race of Gaelic-speaking Scots came to these shores from Ireland; indeed, until the nineteenth century the Gaelic language was almost invariably referred to by southerners as Erse or Irish.

KERR This is the Scots form of Carr, and comes from an Old Norse word *kjarr* meaning brushwood. Kerr is therefore a locality name, although there is no settlement of that name nowadays.

Carr was a common spelling in fifteenth- and sixteenth-century Scotland, but the modern form is Ker (the Roxburgh branch of the family) or Kerr (the Lothian branch). There were numerous other branches of the family in the Borders, two of whom (of Ferniehurst and Cessford respectively) vied for the appointment of Warden of the

Middle March (a lucrative border-policeman post) until they were united by marriage in 1631. From the union derive the earldom and marquessate of Lothian, and the earldom and dukedom of Roxburgh.

There grew up a legend that the Kerrs were left-handed, and built their spiral staircases with a left-hand thread for better defence by south-paw swordsmen. A derivation of the name Kerr (from the Gaelic *cearr* meaning wrong) has been devised as evidence, but there is nothing in history, etymology or even common sense to support this notion.

KING The prevalence of this name in Scotland as elsewhere is something of an enigma, for its bearers have never claimed royal descent. A possible theory is that names such as King, Prince, Pope, Lord, Knight and Page derive from the fact that in the Middle Ages each town held its pageants and processions and presented its folk plays, in which the roles were enacted year after year by the same persons. The nicknames tended to become surnames.

Another favourite character in medieval folk plays was the Abbot of Unreason. This may well be the origin of the Lowland surname Abbott, bearing in mind that real-life medieval abbots would be celibate.

L

LAMONT If the stress is put on the first syllable, as it ought to be, the meaning ('lawman, lawgiver') becomes much clearer. The specious French derivation from *la monte* may be dismissed; the name Lamont or Lamond is from Old Norse *logmadr*, and passed into Gaelic as *laomainn*. MacClymont is from the same source.

The progenitor of the clan Lamont was of the royal house of Dalriada and in the early Middle Ages the clan held large tracts of land in Argyll. An inscription in the ancient churchyard of Kilmun refers to 'the great MacLamond of all Cowal'.

But, alas, the Royalist Lamonts fell foul of the Whig

Campbells, and after a particularly bloody massacre in 1646 'all Cowal' became the domain of the latter clan.

LINDSAY Lindsey means Lincoln's Island, and was an  administrative district in that English shire. The first of the name in Scotland was Sir Walter de Lindeseya, whose father had accompanied David I on his return north to Scotland in the early twelfth century. The name Lindsay—albeit with 200 different recorded spellings—subsequently became one of the most notable in Scottish history.

The family fell heir to the lands of Crawford; Sir David Lindsay of Crawford and the Byres became one of the Regents of Scotland and perished in 1268 on a Crusade. A subsequent Sir David Lindsay was created Earl of Crawford in 1398, and the line continues to this day.

Another branch of the family, the Crawford-Lindsays, acquired lands in Glenesk in Angus, and Edzell Castle is a tribute at once to the civilised tastes and warlike habits of this Lowland dynasty.

Mac

MacDONALD The forename Donald—it appears to mean 'world mighty'—is of great antiquity and is first recorded in a Roman inscription of A.D. 20 as being the name of an ancient British prince.

The progenitor of the clan Donald had a distinguished ancestry; his grandfather was Somerlad, scourge of the south-west Highlands, and his grandmother was daughter of

Olaf, King of Man. It is from this Donald that modern Mac-Donalds, MacDonnells and Donaldsons claim descent—although it must be allowed that there could have been other and humbler Donalds who begat minor dynasties of their own. Donnelly is an Irish importation, of different linguistic origin.

The first MacDonald possession was Islay; the family became Lords of the Isles, extended their possessions on the mainland by marriage (including a royal alliance), and eventually succeeded to the earldom of Ross. In the chaos which followed the forfeiture of the Lordship of the Isles in 1493, the different branches of the clan developed under their own chiefs. The main branches were of Sleat in Skye, Clanranald in Moidart, Glengarry (with the spelling Macdonnell), Keppoch in Lochaber, and Glencoe.

The MacDonalds were ardent Royalists from the time when Robert the Bruce gave them the honour of taking position on the right wing of the army at Bannockburn, a claim which they still pressed at Culloden 432 years later. The clan suffered grievously under the post-Jacobite repressions and under the maladministration of some of their later chiefs-turned-landlord, and vast migrations to North America took place in the eighteenth and nineteenth centuries. Nevertheless, MacDonald is by far the commonest Mac name in Scotland.

MACDUFF Shakespeare's Macduff was almost certainly a fictitious character, created not by the Bard but by one of the early chroniclers. But there was a historical MacDuff (and like Macbeth his was a forename and not a surname) who was progenitor of the clan and who was second son of the Celtic earl of Fife at the time of Robert the Bruce. This MacDuff may have been descended from the twelfth-century King Duf; but the form Duff (meaning black) has apparently no connection with the earls of Fife.

The main MacDuff line died out in the Middle Ages, and it was on a Banffshire branch of the family that the Victorian dukedom of Fife was bestowed; by this time the family owned no land in Fife. The name MacDuff is now perhaps best known as that of a village on the Moray Firth founded by the latter-day Lords of Fife.

The MacDuffs are interesting as a clan which virtually became extinct under that name. A MacDuff gathering today would muster few adherents; but the clan spawned many others in a way which illustrates the development of clan organisation in the Highlands. The son of an early MacDuff earl became known as *mac an toiseach* (son of the chief) and this designation became the surname MacIntosh. One of the younger MacIntosh sons with the Christian name Shaw ('wolf') branched out to form the clan Shaw. Another MacIntosh son by the name Farquhar acquired a following of his own and formed the clan Farquharson. His descendant Finlay ('fair hero') Farquharson had offspring who took the name MacFhionnlaidh (MacKinlay) or Finlayson. Every stage in the process gave rise to a surname, but who is to say where one clan ended and another began? By the mid-eighteenth century when the clan system finally dis-integrated the picture had become very confused, and it took the tartan-purveyors of the Victorian era to sort it all out into a neat system of clans, septs and families.

MacFARLANE According to ancient Irish mythology, it was Partholon, son of Sear, who took possession of Ireland after the Flood. Be that as it may, Partholon gave his name to the Argyllshire clan MacFarlane, or MacPharlain as it is in Gaelic. The name Partholon has no English equivalent, and is certainly not cognate with Bartholomew.

The MacFarlanes were an offshoot of the ancient Celtic earls of Lennox and received from them a title to lands in Arrochar; they held sway on Loch Long and Loch Sloy (the clan's war cry) until the end of the eighteenth century when, like so many other clans, their estates were sold and the chief emigrated to America. The MacFarlanes are now landless and chiefless.

MacGREGOR In Gaelic, *clann* means simply 'children', and the whole theory of clanship depends on the blood relationship between chief and followers. Even as late as Culloden the chief of the Keppoch MacDonalds rallied his men as 'the children of my tribe'.

However, the notion of blood relationship and of descent from a common ancestor was sometimes a fiction and one that was hard to sustain. Who was the original Gregor from whom the MacGregors descended? Was he, as was once claimed, Griogar the son of Kenneth Macalpine? Or perhaps, as a later and less likely claim had it, Pope Gregory the Great? Whatever the truth may be, all MacGregors claimed a common descent, and a royal one at that.

Clanship was not necessarily based upon ownership of territory. The MacGregors, who hailed from West Perthshire, appear to have lost their clan territories at a very early stage. 'Glenstrae and Glenorchy no longer are ours . . .' runs the lament, but whatever the clan originally possessed was held by the sword and was never feudalised as so many Highland estates were. Yet the landless clan continued to exist as an entity for three centuries, and even in 1745 could muster a clan regiment of 700 men under the leadership of Rob Roy MacGregor's elder son.

After a peculiarly dastardly piece of behaviour in 1603

32

known as the Raid of Glenfruin which resulted in the deaths of a few hundred Colquhouns, the name MacGregor was proscribed 'under the pain of death' (to quote the Act). Charles II removed this penalty in recognition of the clan's services in the Royalist cause, but the luckless MacGregors were again proscribed in the reign of William III. The chief adopted the name Murray, and Rob Roy took his mother's name of Campbell, as readers of Sir Walter Scott will remember. Even in the general amnesty after the '15 Rebellion a specific exclusion was made for the MacGregors, and it was not until 1774 that the ban was lifted. The chief then resumed the family name, and many of his adherents must have done likewise, for there are still many MacGregors in Scotland and beyond—a tribute to the pride and tenacity of a clan who for more than 150 years had been treated as vermin.

The diminutive form Greig also gives a surname (and Edvard Grieg's ancestors are said to be of Highland stock). However, not all Gregorys and Gregsons are Scottish, since Gregory is also an English—and was originally a Greek—name.

MacINTOSH _Toiseach_ in Gaelic meant a tribal leader, equivalent to the later thane and still later feudal baron. MacIntosh therefore means 'son of the leader', and although any leader can be intended it is thought that the first MacIntosh was son of one of the Thanes of Fife (see MacDUFF).

The clan system took its form from the imposition of Anglo-Norman feudalism on to an organisation purely tribal in character. (Although there was no Norman military conquest of Scotland, the early Scottish Kings were not slow to import Anglo-Norman heavyweights to strengthen the central government.) The old Celtic leaders were forced to seek written charters to lands which their ancestors had held by ancient custom. The first MacIntosh was given a charter to lands in the Findhorn valley, and for many centuries the clan were to seek, with varying degrees of success, to establish a legal title to their other ancestral possessions. At one time these ranged from Rothiemurchus in the east to Lochaber in the west.

Today the MacIntosh country is the barony of Moy in Inverness-shire, where the clan chief still resides. It is claimed, however, that the Perthshire MacIntoshes are of different origin, being descended from one Ewan who was granted a thanage by Robert II in the fourteenth century.

As well as occupying an honoured place in Highland history the name MacIntosh also has a curiously mundane association. It was a Charles MacIntosh (1766-1843) who patented the idea of treating cloth with a solution of rubber, thus producing the ever-useful mackintosh. The spelling 'Mackintosh' is much more ancient than waterproofing, and although illogical it has become respectable through very long usage.

MacKAY This is the second commonest Mac name in Scotland and means son of Aodh, for which there is no English equivalent. (It does not mean son of Hugh, which is a Germanic name of totally different origin.) Another version of MacKay is MacGhie, which perhaps gives a better idea of the Gaelic pronunciation of Aodh. Mackie is from the same source, a fact which is obscured by the universal habit of stressing the first syllable.

34

The MacKays, probably of Norse origin, established themselves in the north-west corner of Scotland, and by the fifteenth century there were reckoned to be 4,000 male MacKays of military age. The clan in later times was staunchly Protestant, and a MacKay chief took 3,000 men to fight for Gustavus Adolphus in the Thirty Years War. From this German expedition came the famous prints of MacKay warriors in Highland dress, among the earliest illustrations of kilted soldiery.

The MacKay chief was elevated to the peerage as Lord Reay (the name of the clan territory, and itself a surname); but despite being ennobled by a Catholic Stewart sovereign the clan continued to support the Protestant succession. It was Hugh MacKay of Scourie who commanded the troops of William of Orange at Killiecrankie, and in both of the Jacobite rebellions the MacKays were in arms against the Stewarts. (It is sometimes forgotten that there was very little military support for Charles Edward north of Dingwall and south of Perth.)

In the early nineteenth century the MacKays, always vulnerable to their powerful neighbours the Earls of Sutherland, were obliged to part with their vast possessions. The raising of the MacKay Highlanders, and the Kildonan and Strathnaver clearances completed the dispersal of this once highly localised clan.

MacKENZIE MacKenzie is son of Coinneach, meaning fair or bright, a Celtic forename which has been taken to be cognate with Kenneth. The name used to be pronounced 'Mack-aing-ye', the 'z' (see MENZIES) being an orthographical peculiarity; but nobody now uses the correct pronunciation.

The clan MacKenzie rose to rapid prominence in the north-west Highlands after the forfeiture of the Lordship of the Isles in 1493, only to fall again with the passing of the Stewart dynasty. The sons of Coinneach the Fair gave their name to two earldoms, a barony and several landed proprietors, and to hundreds of thousands of ordinary Scots throughout the ages. They must have been a prolific clan— their fighting strength in 1745 was reckoned to be 2,500 and they later provided most of the manpower for the Seaforth Highlanders—and even today MacKenzie is the commonest Mac name after MacDonald and MacKay.

MacLACHLAN Lachlan was a favourite Celtic forename, coming from the Gaelic word *Lochlann* meaning Norway. The clan MacLachlan claims descent from Niall of the Nine Hostages, who was High King of Ireland and was granted lands in Argyllshire. The clan has had a happier history than many, for although they participated in all the available Royalist and Jacobite wars they contrived to keep on good terms with their powerful Campbell neighbours and avoided the worst of the after-effects of the '45. Although so many Highland clans are now landless and chiefless, one is happy to be able to record that the 24th Chief, MacLachlan of MacLachlan still lives at Castle Lachlan in Strathlachlan. Reverence for the family name could scarcely go further.

MacLEAN In 1390 Donald, Lord of the Isles, granted extensive lands in Morven and the Inner Hebrides to his two MacLean brothers-in-law. From this stock came the two main branches of the clan: the MacLeans of Duart, and the MacLaines of Lochbuie. Duart and Lochbuie are both in Mull, and Dr Johnson when visiting that island in 1773 remarked that in this country every man's name is MacLean; he might almost say the same today.

The clan is known in Gaelic as *Clan Gillean*, and this gives a clue to the etymology—*Mac gille Eoin*, son of the servant of St John. Names with *gille* in them have a dedicatory function (see GILCHRIST), and when this element is combined with *Mac* it tends to be gobbled up either in the prefix or the stem

of the name. Thus, MacLehose is a contraction of *Mac gille Thoimis*, son of the servant of St Thomas; MacLellan is *Mac gille Fhillan*, of St Fillan; MacLagan is a follower of Adamnan; and MacLees and MacLeish are shortened forms of *Mac gille Iosa*, son of the follower of Jesus. On a secular level, but still preserving the *gille* element are MacLure (*Mac gille odhar*—son of the dun-coloured lad); MacAvoy (*mac gille bhuidh*—son of the yellow-haired lad); and MacIlroy and MacIlraith (*mac gille rhuadh*—son of the red-headed lad).

MacLEOD Many of the clans of the north and west Highlands were of Norse origin, and the MacLeods are perhaps the most important. The name comes from *Liotr*, which was Gaelicised to Leod and pronounced 'Lodge' in Gaelic. The Leod in question is supposed to have been son of the Norse King of Man and the Hebrides, who was given lands in Lewis. Another branch of the clan acquired lands in Skye, and to these were added the island of Raasay and lands in Assynt and Strathpeffer (where they built Castle Leod, later to fall into the hands of the MacKenzies of Cromarty).

The MacLeods, weary of royal ingratitude, remained on the side-lines during the Jacobite rebellions and escaped the worst consequences of the post-Culloden reprisals; had they not, Dunvegan Castle (which the MacLeods have occupied for 700 years) might today be in the ruinous state of Invergarry and many other castles.

Other Norse personal names which give rise to clan surnames are Hromund (MacCrimmon—the hereditary piper to the MacLeods); Magnus (MacManus); Olaf (MacAulay); and Sven (MacQueen). But the most interesting of these, reeking of barbaric idolatry, is Thorkettil (Thor's cauldron) which passes into English as Thirkell and into Gaelic as MacCorquodale.

MacMILLAN   The name means, like it or not, 'son of the little bald one'. But see MALCOLM for an explanation of the baldness; and the 'little' is probably an affectionate term rather than an indication of size, so a better translation of *Mac Mhaolain* might be 'son of the beloved priest'.

The family of the original Maolan acquired territories in Argyll, and built the ancient fortress of Castle Sween in Knapdale. The clan burial ground is in Kilmory churchyard near by, and a huge stone cross bearing the legend 'Haec est crux Alexandri Mac Millan' commemorates the builder of Castle Sween.

Like many another Argyll clan the MacMillans lost their lands to the Campbells. One branch took refuge with the Camerons in Lochaber. The stewards of Lochaber at that time were MacIntoshes, while the district was the hereditary domain of the clan Cameron; so that the Lochaber MacMillans lived as tenants of the MacIntoshes but as adherents of the Camerons, and in the event of a fight between the MacIntoshes and the Camerons (a frequent occurrence) it was anybody's guess which side the MacMillans would take—a pleasing example of the clan system as it was in unromantic reality.

Other branches of the clan appear on Loch Tay side,

where the name is still found. The ancestors of Mr Harold Macmillan came from the Island of Arran.

Mullan and Mulligan have the same derivation as Mac-Millan, but are Irish versions of the name which reached Scotland in the nineteenth-century immigrations.

MacPHEE   Scots of the older generation will associate the name MacPhee with bands of tinkers living in various encampments on the fringes of the Highlands. Yet the origin of this clan is romantic enough. The name comes from the ancient forename *Dubhshith*—the dark fairy—and appears in twelfth-century Iona as *MacDhubhsith*, later contracted to MacDuffie (no connection with MacDUFF, q.v.) and later still as MacFie or MacPhee.

The MacPhees established themselves on the island of Colonsay, but with the murder of their chief in 1623 the clan broke up and dispersed over the mainland. The MacPhees are the classic type of the broken clan, landless and chiefless and finding protection wherever they might. Some of them attached themselves to the Clan Cameron and ended their days with Lochiel's regiment on Culloden Moor. In the following century, one Ewen MacPhee encamped with his family on an island in Loch Quoich, living as a sort of Victorian Rob Roy without regard to law or landowner; it may have been from him that the vagrant MacPhees were descended.

In the Lowlands the name was sometimes shortened to Duffie (not to be confused with Duthie, which is a contraction for St Duthac).

MacPHERSON   This is the surname of a famous clan in Badenoch, one of the confederation known as Clan Chattan. The name means son of the parson, and is a clerical patronymic which pre-dates the Reformation by several centuries. The old Celtic church had a tradition of a hereditary priesthood, and this survived in parts of the Highlands almost until the introduction of a non-celibate ministry with the Reformation. Other examples of Highland clerical names are MacVicar, MacTaggart (*mac an t-sagairt*, son of the priest) and MacNab (son of the abbot). The English cognates of Parsons, Vickers and Priest are not found in Lowland Scotland.

The clan originated in Lochaber but were granted lands in Badenoch by a grateful Robert the Bruce for their services in helping to destroy his enemies the Comyns or Cummings who had previously ruled in Strathspey. The MacPhersons themselves are now in turn dispersed and dispossessed, but their traditions are preserved in the beautiful countryside of Kingussie, Laggan and Loch Ericht.

MacRAE The clan known as 'the wild MacRaes' held office under the MacKenzies of Kintail and were hereditary Constables of Eilan Donan Castle on Loch Duich. It was a descendant of the MacRaes who was responsible for the restoration of the castle, surely the most picturesque fortress in the Highlands.

MacRae means 'son of grace', and its alternative forms MacCraw, MacRath and MacGrath are nearer to the Gaelic original. Not all Mac names embody the idea of 'son of' in a literal sense. Just as American English has 'son of a gun' or gangster, so Gaelic more poetically has *mactallamh* meaning 'son of the rocks', or echo, and *macmollachd* meaning 'son of a curse' or devil. MacRae is a name of this type, and so are MacBeth ('son of life') and MacGillivray ('son of a devotee of judgement'). On a more mundane level we have Mac-Sporran, which is a genuine name and not a music-hall one, and means 'son of a purse' or bursar, and MacLung which means 'son of a ship' or sailor.

M

MALCOLM In a primitive society names have a magical quality, and the early Gaels were extremely careful to choose propitious names for their offspring (see GILCHRIST). The ancient way of expressing a sense of dedication was to use the

Gaelic word *maol* meaning bald or tonsured, and to say that a child was 'the tonsured one of Jesus'. This gives the name Malise (*maol Iosa*) which was a common Highland Christian name and gives us Mollison. The Irish names Muldoon, Mulcahey and Mulholland preserve the same idea.

But by far the commonest name of this type is Malcolm (*maol Colm*) which means devotee of St Columba. (Columba is the Latinised form of the Gaelic Colm, meaning dove.) Malcolm occurred as a surname in Dunbartonshire in the fourteenth century, and the family appears to have moved south to Dumfriesshire. Although Malcolm was the name of four early Scottish kings and was always popular at the font, it did not become common as a surname until comparatively late in the day.

There has been much confusion between this name and  that of MacCallum, particularly since the chief of the MacCallums, with more *pietas* than scholarship, changed his name to Malcolm. MacCallum probably means son of Cailean (simplified to Callum), which is taken to be cognate with Colin.

MARSHALL The French word *maréchal* means farrier or shoesmith. It came to Britain with the Normans, and a horse-servant became in time a hereditary office of great importance similar to Constable and Steward. One Philip Marescallus married the ancestress of Keith-Humbie, and became the progenitor of the Keith family who rose to great fame as Earls Marischall of Scotland.

Most of the Scottish Marshalls, however, are likely to be of humbler origin, deriving their surname from the once all-important occupation of horse-servant or groom. In the Middle Ages there must have been more grooms than there are garage attendants today, and it is not surprising that Marshall is now among the sixty most frequent Scottish surnames.

MARTIN Mars was the pagan god of war, and gave his name to the Christian apostle St Martin of Tours. St Martin was greatly honoured in Normandy and at least twenty-five places bear his name. It is uncertain whether the Martins of this island brought the place-name with them from Normandy or simply adopted the personal name, but the surname has become very common both in England and Scotland.

St Martin was also revered among the Gaels, and the name *Mac Gille Mhartainn* (meaning son of the devotee of Martin, and later becoming MacMartin) is recorded. The clan MacMartin of Letterfinlay were powerful in Lochaber, but their lands passed by marriage to the Camerons, whose banner they followed and under whose protection they came; no doubt many a MacMartin also adopted the Cameron surname on leaving his home territory.

MATHESON This name has both a Lowland and a Highland form, and it is quite impossible to tell from the spelling which is which. The Lowland form is son of Matthew ('gift of God') and is sometimes spelt Matthewson. Since Matthew was a favourite Christian name, the surname Matheson belongs to no particular district but is found all over the Lowlands. The form Matthews is usually Welsh, but Mathieson, Massie and Masson are not infrequent in Scotland.

The Highland form of the name is much more localised, for the Mathesons held lands of the medieval earls of Ross. The clan territory is traditionally that part of the mainland of

Wester Ross which faces Skye, but they later spread to the islands and to Sutherland. A latter-day Matheson acquired many of the MacLeod lands in Lewis.

The Highland Mathesons were originally *Mac Mathain* ('son of the bear') and other Gaelic forms of the name are MacMath and MacMahon, the latter being very common in Ireland.

MENZIES The interesting linguistic feature of this name is the letter 'z' which is really an obsolete letter yogh (3) representing something between a 'y' and a 'g' sound. The name is usually pronounced correctly in Scotland ('Ming-iz'), but barbarities like 'Men-zaze' are all too frequently heard. A similar formation is found in Dalziel and Gilzean, with the same pronunciation hazards.

The name came from Mèsnieres in Normandy, via England (where its cognate is Manners, the family name of the dukes of Rutland). Menzies is a good example of an Anglo-Norman family which received a grant of Scottish land under royal patronage and founded a clan based not so much on the idea of kindred as on feudal tenure. These clans, despite their alien origin, became thoroughly Gaelicised, and were fiercely proud of the Celtic past of their adopted country.

The Menzies clan is now associated principally with the lands of Weem in Strathtay, where their ancient castle is in process of being restored by the Clan Society.

MILLER One of the top ten Scottish surnames in popularity, and the third commonest occupational one after Smith and Stewart. The name must have sprung up all over the Lowlands wherever corn was ground and it belongs to no particular locality. The Gaelic version of miller would be *muillear,* but this does not appear to have given rise to a distinctive surname unless it be that the characteristic Scottish spelling 'Millar' shows a Highland origin.

The English forms Milner and Millward are not found in Scotland, but the location-name Milne (at the mill) is very common here. Millin and Millen are versions of the same, and indicate the vernacular pronunciation, but do not confuse these with MacMillan (q.v.).

MITCHELL The Hebrew name Michael means 'who is like the Lord?' and was a common baptismal name throughout Christendom. It appears to have come to Britain in its softened French form of Michel; the Scots, however, have always had a fine disregard for the correct pronunciation of foreign words, and the name became naturalised here as Mitchell, first as a forename and then as a surname. (They say that even today Michael is pronounced Mitchell in Orkney.)

A version of the name in its diminutive form is found in Angus and Aberdeenshire in the name Michie and is said to have originated in Glengairn, where a Michael MacDonald of the Keppoch branch of that clan founded a family in the sixteenth century.

The forms MacMichael and MacMichie are both recorded, but are comparatively rare. The name Carmichael is different, being a place-name originally: *caer* is Brythonic for fort (as in Caernarvon), and Carmichael was the name of a settlement in Lanarkshire.

MORRISON The Christian name Maurice (from Latin *mauricius* meaning Moorish or swarthy) was brought to Britain by the Normans and anglicised to Morris. It is not native to Scotland in that form, but appears as the surname Morrison or Morison, and belongs to no particular area.

There is also a Highland version of the name, spelt in the same way, but with a completely different derivation; it is a reduction of *Mac ghille Mhuire*—son of the Virgin Mary's servant. *Mhuire-son* becomes Murison (an Aberdeenshire name), while if the *Mac* is dropped one gets *Gille Mhuire* or Gilmour. The Hebridean Morrisons may alternatively have come from an Irish family of O Murcheasain ('descendant of the mariner').

A Scottish Morrison may therefore have an ancestor who

was a son of Maurice, of a sailor, or of a devotee of the Virgin; the first of the three is the most likely.

MUNRO There is a firm tradition (supported by doubtful etymology) that the Munros came originally from the mouth of the River Roe (Bun Rotha) in Ireland. Historically, they are found in Easter Ross from the fourteenth century, where the chiefs were known as the Munros of Foulis. They were one of the many Whig clans (like the Campbells, the Mac-Kays and the Grants) who supported the Government in the Jacobite rebellions. It is not always remembered that in 1745 more Scots bore arms against Prince Charles than supported him.

Several Munro clansmen were transported to America in the seventeenth century, having incurred the displeasure of Cromwell, and the clan flourished there. Two of its members are of particular note: one of them fired the first shot in the War of Independence; another became President of the United States of America.

MURPHY This, of course, is not a Scottish surname at all. It is by far the commonest name in Ireland, however, and by immigration has become one of the seventy commonest in Scotland, particularly in the industrial west. It must be included here for that reason, but it is also interesting because it connects with other names which are purely Scottish.

Murphy comes from *O Murchada*, which is Irish Gaelic for 'descendant of the sea-warrior'. The native Scottish form is *Mac Murchadh*, which becomes Murchison and Murchie, common at one time throughout the Highlands. *Murchadh* became inextricably confused with another Gaelic forename *Muireach* (meaning mariner) which gives the Scottish names MacMurdo and Murdoch. The confusion does not exist in Ireland, where *Muireach* takes the modern form of Moriarty.

MURRAY This is the commonest locality or territorial name in Scotland, and comes from the province or shire of

Moray ('seaboard settlement'). The original William of Moray owned lands there, and his descendants extended their possessions southwards; one of them, Andrew Murray, died after supporting William Wallace's army at Stirling Bridge.

In the Middle Ages, the standard way of acquiring property was by marriage rather than by warfare (this was true even in the Highlands), and by this means the various branches of the Murray family became possessed of the lands of Abercairney and Tullibardine in eastern Perthshire. The second Murray earl of Tullibardine married a Stewart heiress of Atholl, and in time the Murray chiefs became Dukes of Atholl. Others of the Tullibardine line founded separate dynasties, including Stormont and Ochtertyre. These are all places in Perthshire, and the name Murray might be expected to be commoner there than it in fact is; however, despite the Murray dukedom of Atholl, there are still more Stewarts than Murrays in the area.

N

NICOLL This is a diminutive of Nicholas, a personal name introduced to Britain by the Normans. It is derived from Greek, and means 'victorious people'. Of all the surnames derived from Nicholas the most common in Scotland are Nicol, Nichol and Nicoll; they appear all over the coun-

try from the sixteenth century onwards. The English forms Nicholls and Nixon are not found in medieval Scotland.

The Highland branch of the family seem to have used the names MacNicol and Nicolson more or less at random. They became established in the north-west Highlands at a very early period, and although their lands eventually passed to the MacLeods, the name is still frequently found in Skye. It was Sheriff Nicholson of Portree who named some of the Cuillin peaks in the nineteenth century.

The Nicolsons of Lasswade, Midlothian, were an ancient family, knighted in the seventeenth century. An eighteenth-century Sir William Nicolson was married four times and fathered twenty-three children—thus do surnames proliferate.

O

OGILVIE This em-
bodies the same Brythonic
word as occurs in Ochil,
and means a high plain.
Ogilvie (or *Ocel Fa* as it
originally was) was a Pictish province in Angus
(there is still a Glen Ogilvie near Glamis) and the
property was settled on
Gillebride, second son of
the Earl of Angus. Gil-
lebride Normanised his
name to Gilbert, and took
a new surname from his
Ogilvie estates. The fam-
ily became hereditary
sheriffs of Angus, and one
of them was killed at the
Red Harlaw in 1411. His
descendant was created
Lord Ogilvie of Airlie in

1491, and an earldom followed a century later. Always a royalist family, the Ogilvies provided a regiment in 1745 under the command of the young son of the 4th earl. Of the 600 men enlisted twenty-three bore the surname Ogilvie. Other names of the soldiers were Edward, Anderson, Smith and Robertson—all of which names still predominate in the district of Angus where the Airlie estates are located.

P

PATERSON Patrick was as popular a Christian name in Scotland as in Ireland, and Paterson is among the twenty-five most frequently found Scottish surnames. The spelling

with the single 't' is commoner in Scotland, the double 't' being found in the north of England. The characteristic Scottish glottal stop results all too frequently in the 't' not being pronounced at all.

The common diminutive of Patrick was Pate (also a Scottish surname), and this gives the double diminutive form Paton, a name once common in the Angus village of Usan almost to the exclusion of all others. Paton, originally a Lowland Christian name, strayed across the Highland line and became popular with Gaelic-speaking families. As a surname it took the form MacFadzean; a good instance of a Mac surname which is not a clan name. Other examples are MacRobbie, MacWattie and McGibbon, which originated on the Highland boundary where Lowland personal names were heard by Gaelic speakers.

Patrick itself becomes Padruig in Gaelic, and the son of Patrick appears in the curious spelling of McFetridge or MacPartridge, an oddity comparable with MacCambridge, which is an attempt to indicate 'son of Ambrose'.

PATTULLO This is by no means a common Scottish surname, but it is an interesting one linguistically. It is a locality name from the lands of Pittilloch in Fife, and the first three letters preserve the word *peit* which meant piece or part and is the characteristic settlement word of the Picts. (The word *peit* or *pit* passed into Gaelic with a particular anatomical meaning. Latter-day Gaels became squeamish about its use, and even now Pitlochry in Gaelic is rendered *Baile Chloichrigh*.) The second half of the name is the Gaelic *tulach*, which means little hill, so that Pattullo is 'the knoll-place'. Tullo, Tulloch, Tullis and Tough are all surnames with the same derivation.

Although 'Pit' place-names are abundant in Scotland in the areas settled by the Picts (i.e. Fife, Angus, east Perthshire and Aberdeenshire), they give rise to surprisingly few surnames. But Pitcairn (the rock place), Pitcaithly ('Cathalan's place'), Pitbladdo (the meal place) and Pittendreich (the place of the aspect) are all in the telephone directory.

R

RAMSAY Here we have yet another example of a thoroughly Scottish name which is of English origin. There is, or was, a place in Huntingdonshire called Ramsey, which means 'wild garlic island'. In the twelfth century, one Simund de Ramesie moved north and his family became established in Scotland, later acquiring the estates of Dalhousie in Midlothian.

The Ramsays played a significant part in the Wars of Independence, and William of Dalhousie was a signatory of the Declaration of Arbroath in 1320. The family became earls of Dalhousie in 1633, and took the Whig side in the politics of the following century; they are still notable landowners in Angus, having inherited the Panmure estates.

Allan Ramsay the poet, and his even more distinguished son Allan Ramsay the painter, have made the name famous in the annals of Scottish culture.

REID Both the spelling and pronunciation of the word 'red' are modern; in pre-surname times the 'e' was long, and the spelling was 'reed' in England and 'reid' in Scotland. The surname Reid therefore means red-haired or florid in complexion.

Reid is the fourteenth commonest surname in Scotland, and although most frequently found in Ayrshire it is now fairly evenly distributed. Some Reids may, however, have a Highland origin, for the Gaelic word for red is *ruadh*, and General Reid of the Reid School of Music was descended from Alastair Ruadh of Strathardle. Reid is also found in the north of England, but the characteristic English form is Reed or Read.

Another name which expresses ruddiness of skin or hair is Russell, which is a diminutive of the Old French word *ros*, meaning red. Although Russell is basically an English name, it has been recorded in Scotland since the twelfth century and is still among the fifty commonest names in this country.

ROBERTSON   This name is found with great frequency in the Perth and Dundee districts, and many of its bearers are no doubt descended from the Perthshire Clan Donnachaidh (see DUNCAN) whose clan surname was Robertson. Robert, grandson of Duncan of Glenerochy, had his Struan lands erected into a barony in 1451; and the Robertsons of Struan were among the most ardent and persistent Jacobites of later centuries. Alasdair, the 17th chief, scored a hat-trick by taking up arms for the Stewarts in 1689, 1715 and 1745. There are still Robertsons in Rannoch, but the chiefly line is no longer there and the lands have been sold.

Robertsons are almost equally common in England, so it is not safe to assume that if one bears the name one's origins are in Perthshire. There must have been many an early medieval Robert (it means 'fame bright') whose name was bestowed on his progeny. The forms Roberts and Robinson are not native to Scotland, nor is the rhyming diminutive Hob (which gives the English surnames Hobbes, Hobson, Hopkins and Hopkinson), but we do have Dobbie and Dobson in this country. Bob must be a modern contraction, for it gives no surname. Robson and Robison were recorded in Caithness from early times.

MacRobert and MacRobb are Gaelic versions current in Aberdeenshire and apparently have no connection with the Perthshire Robertsons.

ROSS   It is a curious fact that whereas in England places tend to be called after people, in Scotland it is the other way about. There are very many locality-surnames in Scotland, and one of the most notable is Ross. It comes from the Gaelic word *ros*, meaning promontory, and the clan territory was that point of land known until regionalisation as Easter Ross.

The ancient Celtic earldom of Ross dated from the thirteenth century; it reverted to the crown on the forfeiture of the Lordship of the Isles in 1476. It then became a royal dukedom under the early Stewarts but eventually died out. Meanwhile the chiefship of the clan Ross had devolved on the Rosses of Balnagowan near Tain, whose lands were in turn sold in the eighteenth century.

It is unlikely that all present-day Rosses had their family origin in the north-east; there must have been more than one *ros* (i.e. promontory) in Gaelic-speaking Scotland which gave rise to the surname.

The name Ross must be distinguished from that of the neighbouring family of Rose of Kilravock, whose origin is as thoroughly Norman as its subsequent history is Highland.

RUTHERFORD   It used to be a legend that this name originated with a band of cattle thieves who were apprehended while wading a river and therefore had cause to 'rue the ford'. Fortunately this type of bogus etymology is no longer taken seriously; the name actually comes from the lands of Rutherford in Roxburghshire and has much the same meaning as Oxford (Old English *hrythera* means 'horned cattle'). There is in existence a thirteenth-century seal of one Mestre de Rotherforde which bears a wild bull's head with prominent horns, suggesting that the true derivation of the name was known at that time.

S

SCOTT   This is a racial rather than a locality name, and dates from the time when non-Scottish inhabitants of this land (in the form of Britons, Angles and Norsemen) were still clearly identifiable. The origin of the name Scott is fairly widespread in the Lowlands, although it later came to be associated mainly with Border families, the chief of which became the Dukes of Buccleuch. Sir Walter Scott, although a typical product of the Edinburgh enlightenment, was descended from the ancient Border line of Scott of

Harden—a circumstance from which he derived much satisfaction.

Certain types of name gain currency only when the bearer leaves home; nobody has the nickname Taffy in Wales itself. So an English family moving north might acquire the surname Inglis; an immigrant Norwegian might be called Norrie, and a man from Flanders might be known as Fleming (q.v.). Other examples are Charteris (from Chartres), Danskin (from Danzig) and Bremner (from Brabant). If the point of origin was unknown, the incomer might simply receive the name Strang.

SIMPSON   The name Simon (despite, apparently, meaning hyena) has once again become a popular Christian name, having fallen from favour for a few centuries. Its diminutive was Sim, and gives the surname Simson or Simpson, the 'p' being what phonologists are pleased to call a parasitic glide consonant.

Simpson is a Lowland name which did not reach any great prominence until the nineteenth century when the use of chloroform made famous the name of Sir James Simpson, the great Edinburgh physician.

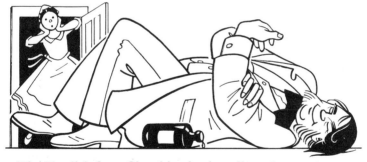

The English form Simpkins is virtually unknown here, as are Simms and Simmonds. Syme and Sime are common enough forms of the diminutive in Scotland. The Gaelic form MacShimi is confined to the chiefly designation or patronymic of the Frasers of Lovat, although the phonetic form MacKimmie is recorded.

SINCLAIR The uncompromising method of pronouncing this name in Scotland ('Sinkler') obscures its origin in St Clair (originally St Clair sur Elle in Normandy). Contractions of Saint names are uncommon in Scotland; although the English name Semple comes from St Paul, the Scots Sempill comes from 'simple' (not necessarily a pejorative nickname).

The Sinclair family became, by marriage, Earls of Orkney and later of Caithness, where the name is still frequently found. As well as being the family name of the earls of Caithness and of four other peers, it is still among the sixty most common Scottish surnames.

STEVENSON Stephen comes from a Greek word meaning wreath or garland and is a biblical name first brought to these shores by the Normans, with whom it was a great favourite. In Scotland the form Steven is preferred, and Stevenson is the commonest form of the patronymic. (Stephenson and Stephens are the characteristic English versions.) Steven does not give rise to a Mac name, but MacStiofan is known in Ireland. The form Stiven is found in Aberdeenshire and Angus.

STEWART After Smith, this is the commonest of the Scottish surnames derived from an occupation. Etymologically, Stewart is *stig-ward*, and although *stig* is cognate with 'sty' it really means hall, and the office of steward became an important and hereditary one. Just as the count of the stable became Constable, the bottler became Butler (the family name of five Irish peers) and the door-ward became Dorward.

The ancestors of the Stewarts were Anglo-Norman re-exports to Scotland who acquired the dignity of High Stewards of the realm. One of them married Marjorie, daughter of Robert the Bruce, and his grandson became Robert II. The numerous royal descendants founded branches of the family in such places as Atholl and Strathearn in Perthshire, Appin in Argyll, Menteith and Strathspey. But not all

54

Stewarts are Royal Stewarts, any more than all stewards are High Stewards, and it may well be that many a humble Lowland steward gave his occupational name to a family. The version Stuart became popular with Mary, Queen of Scots and is, of course, a French spelling, there being no letter 'w' indigenous to that language.

T

TAYLOR A tailor was originally a cutter-out of cloth (from Old French *tailler*, to cut). The name occurs in Scots records from the earliest times (occasionally alternating with its Latinised version, Scissor, now alas unknown), and is among the twenty commonest in Scotland. It must be added, however, that it is even more common south of the Border.

The word tailor passed into Gaelic as *taillear*, and gave rise to a Highland version of the surname, *Macantaillear*, which however did not suffer transplanting in the Lowlands and reverted to its original form of Taylor. Based on the flimsy evidence of the existence of one *Taillear dubh*, who was a follower of Cameron of Lochiel, it has been widely maintained that the Taylors are a sept of the clan Cameron. This will not stand up to examination, and the truth is that most Scottish Taylors are descended from one or other of the many practitioners of the humble but necessary trade of tailoring, whether in the Highlands or the Lowlands or even in England.

THOMSON The third most frequent surname in Scotland, and a commoner patronymic even than MacDonald. The prevalence of the surname illustrates that Thomas was a very popular Christian name in the early Middle Ages. Indeed, with our wide variety of modern forenames, we are inclined to forget that in the Lowlands most names were either Norman (William, Robert, Archibald), or biblical (John, James, Thomas and David). The royal Christian names of Kenneth, Malcolm and Duncan were popular, as were the saintly ones of Patrick, Mungo and Ninian. That just about exhausts the list; only comparatively recently did Gaelic names like Ian, Alastair, Angus and Colin become popular in the Lowlands. Of girls' names the most popular was Jean (with its diminutive Janet), followed by Agnes, Ann, Elizabeth (in its form Elspeth), Isobel and Margaret, none of which, for obvious reasons, gives a surname (see BELL).

Thomsons are found all over Lowland Scotland, and the name has its Gaelic equivalent in MacThomas, a small clan which had lands in Glenshee until ousted by a series of clan battles and lawsuits in the seventeenth century. Some of these Glenshee MacThomases (or MacComishes) may have changed their name to Thomson on emigrating to the Lowlands, but the idea that all Thomsons are of the Glenshee stock is quite absurd. This did not prevent the formation in recent years of a Clan Thomas Society, whose elastic membership no doubt includes Welsh Thomases as well as English Tompkinsons.

The diminutive Tommy and the Scotticised Tammas give us MacCombie and MacTavish respectively. Thompson tends to be an English version (the fifteenth commonest surname there), and the 'p' is a glide consonant typical of English phonology.

TURNBULL   The picturesque and persistent legend is that a doughty Borderer saved the life of King Robert the Bruce by diverting a bull by main force from its intention of molesting the royal person. Thereafter, says the historian Boece, the king endowed him with great possessions and his lineage to this day is called Turnbull. There are several drawbacks to this theory, however, one being that the name is recorded before the days of Robert I, and another that this legend is one of the recurrent motifs of Celtic mythology. Perhaps most telling is the fact that this is just not how people get surnames; in 99 per cent of cases surnames are acquired in a quite natural and humdrum way, and very rarely are they imposed as a result of some happening or other, however dramatic.

56

The true origin of the name Turnbull is probably the Old English adjective *trumball*, which means strong or bold. The fact that the family coat of arms of the Turnbulls features a bull need not reinforce belief in the legend, for heraldry is the favourite playground of the punster and scant attention is paid to etymology. For example, the Bell family adopted bells as their motif (Bell means 'fair' and has nothing to do with campanology); and the Oliphants adopted an elephant instead of olives as their heraldic device.

U

URQUHART Urquhart probably comes from two Brythonic words *air* and *cairdean*, meaning 'at the woods', and is the name of a district on the north-west shore of Loch Ness, dominated by the spectacular Castle Urquhart.

As happened so often in Scotland, the family of Urquhart took a name from its place of origin. William of Urquhart became hereditary sheriff of Cromarty during the reign of Robert the Bruce, and the family was knighted under Charles II. Sir Thomas Urquhart (1611-60) claimed to trace his descent from Adam, was a brilliant translator of Rabelais, and is said to have died of convulsive laughter (joyous or Rabelaisian?) on hearing of the Restoration.

The line of Urquharts of Cromartie died out in the eighteenth century and the lands were sold. But the name

lingers in the north-east Highlands and has been transplanted to America, sometimes in the barbarous form Urghad. The early Highland *émigrés* were probably illiterate and took with them only the sound of their surnames. This accounts for the bizarre versions of Highland names that are to be found in North America. Other choice examples are Furguson, Cahoun, McCloud, Chissim and McGlauflin. In England, too, bad spelling has distorted McLaren into McClarence, obscuring the descent from Laurence and substituting Clarence, a name totally unknown to the Gaels.

W

WALKER   Not somebody who walks, but somebody who 'waulks', i.e. treads cloth in the process known as fulling. This is an obsolete trade which must have been very important at one time, judging by the fact that Walker is among the twenty-five commonest Scottish surnames (it is also very frequently found in England).

If your name ends in '-er' or '-ar' it is likely to be an occupational one; and some very odd trades are commemorated in surnames. Here are a few: Jenner (military engineer); Napier (keeper of linen); Ferrier (either ferryman or farrier); Lorimer (spur-maker); Sellar or Sillars (silversmith); Soutar (shoemaker); Tasker (piece-worker); Telfer (iron-cutter, cf. *taille-fer* and Eisenhauer); Collier (charcoal-burner); Crerar (sievewright) and Scrimgeour (skirmisher). These are all from Scots or English words. Gaelic gives us Dewar (pilgrim); Clacher (stone-mason); Grewar (brewer); Grassick (cobbler); Caird (tinker); and Baird (bard or poet).

Our remote ancestors were all hunters, but to judge from the popularity of the surname Hunter (thirty-second in Scotland) many of our more recent ancestors must have lived by this profession also.

WALLACE   Before the gradual unification of the kingdom under Kenneth MacAlpin and his successors there are five distinct ethnic groups to be recognised in the northern part of the British Isles. These are the original Picts, whom Tacitus described; the Scots settlers from Ireland; the Angles from the Kingdom of Northumbria (which at one time stretched to the Lothians and would have gone much farther had the Angles not lost the battle of Nectansmere); the Norse or Viking settlers from Scandinavia (who were much more than just hit-and-run raiders); and the proto-Welsh from the British kingdom of Strathclyde, who were the northern remnant of the 'ancient Britons'.

One of the few discernible benefits of twentieth-century regionalisation is that the name of the ancient kingdom of Strathclyde is once again a household word in Scotland. The capital of this kingdom was Dumbarton ('fort of the Britons') and its inhabitants were of the Brythonic or Welsh race. In the Middle Ages this word became *Wallenses*, and the adjectival form has produced the surname Wallace.

The celebrated William Wallace—he who figures in that most bloodthirsty of all national anthems 'Scots Wha Hae'—was the descendant of a Strathclyde Briton who held lands in Ayrshire. Not all Wallaces claim descent from that particular stock, but all must have come originally from this corner of Scotland.

WATSON   This, of course, means son of Wat, short for Walter, which is a Germanic name brought over by the

Normans. The alternative Scottish form of the surname is Watt, and the English form of Watts, Watkins and Watkinson were never adopted in this country.

The characteristic Scottish method of adopting a surname from a Christian name is to use it unadorned; thus the surname Adam is Scottish, but Adams tends to be English; Jack is Scottish, Jackson is English; Edward is Scottish, Edwards is English, and so on. Watson, along with Robertson and Wilson and a few others, contravenes but does not disprove the rule.

WEBSTER The first Webster worked at the weaver's trade, not necessarily in Scotland. In the same way, the first Baxter was a baker, the first Brewster a brewer, the first Dempster a 'deemer' (or law-giver) and the first Litster or Lister a dyer. The form '-ster' was an agency suffix in Middle English which by linguistic devaluation has acquired a contemptuous association, as in gangster, punster and pollster. The '-ster' ending appears to have survived longer north of the Border, for the names just mentioned have a characteristic Scottish ring. Note by comparison the unfamiliarity here of some of their English equivalents: Baker, Brewer, Weaver and Dyer.

WEIR This name is ultimately of Norman origin, in the sense that it comes from the place-name Vere, which occurs in Calvados, Manche, Oise and other areas of France. Vere is cognate with the English word weir, meaning 'fish-trap'. Scottish bearers of the name may therefore take the choice between being a descendant of the blue-blooded de Veres, or of someone who dwelt by a dam.

The records show a descendant of one Ralph de Vere as possessing in 1400 the Lanarkshire lands of Blackwood (itself to give rise to a distinguished Scottish family name).

Yet another possible origin of the name is an anglicisation of either MacNair (a name which possibly means *Mac an fhuibhar*, son of the smith, or *Mac Amhaoir*, son of the officer). On the whole, a Lowland origin seems more probable and the name is now widespread throughout the country. Major Weir, the celebrated warlock, was burned for witchcraft in 1670; but the name is otherwise respectable and figures in the peerage as the family name of the Barons Inverforth.

WILSON The Christian name William was common all over the Western world, rivalling John in popularity. In origin it is Germanic, consisting like so many others of two unconnected but warlike words, in this instance 'will' (resolve) and 'helmet'. If the popularity in England of the name William is due to The Conqueror, in Scotland it is because of William the Lion (1165-1214).

Like every common forename, William gave rise to a wide variety of surnames, and Williamson is a common enough form in Scotland (Williams, however, is not native). But by far the most popular version is Wilson, which is the sixth commonest name in Scotland. It is so widespread as to defy categorisation, but is noticeably frequent in Fife and Dundee, where it presents something of a hazard in the telephone directories. The name is also very common in England and America, and no Scottish origin can be assumed without additional evidence.

The other form of the diminutive Bill is a modern usage and gives no surname, but the form Wylie is found in Scottish records as early as the fourteenth century. Wilkie is really a double diminutive, and was also found in Fife, while Willock is found in the Mearns and Aberdeenshire.

MacWilliam is probably a surname of Irish origin; when the English conquerors of Ireland began to speak Irish some of them naturalised their Anglo-Norman names. The 'O' form of Irish patronymic having become obsolete, they simply put a Mac in front. The correct Gaelic form of Mac-William would be MacUilleam, and this gives the form MacCulley.

WRIGHT   Any person who made things, or 'wrought', was liable to be known as a wright, and the word caught on as a surname throughout these islands; in England it often had a specialised prefix, e.g. 'cart-', 'wain-' (wagon), 'sieve-', etc. Wright is now a common surname throughout the British Isles, the compound forms of Cartwright, Wainwright and Sievewright being commoner south of the Border.

The word wright survived longer in general use in Scotland than in the south, and came to have the restricted meaning of joiner. Most of the Scottish Wrights were joiners, and indeed there is no other Scottish surname which commemorates the woodworker's trade; Carpenter and Joiner are both very rare in Scotland. There is, however, a Gaelic word *saor* meaning joiner, and the joiner's son was called *mac an t-saoir*, which is anglicised to MacIntyre (Macateer in Ireland). An Argyll clan, the MacIntyres were, appropriately enough, hereditary foresters to the Stewarts of Lorn. In the '45 they fought, along with the MacColls and others, under the banner of the Stewarts of Appin.

Y

YOUNG   Just as a well-doing American may style himself John Burzle, Junior, in order to refer to the fact that his

father still flourishes, so an early-medieval Scot might have been called John Young. This surname must have originated in order to distinguish father and son when both had the same personal name; and Young, after Brown and Reid, is the most frequent nickname-surname in Scotland. The Gaelic for young is *og*, and gives the less common surname Ogg; the Gaels normally used the Mac forms to express juniority.

The name Younger is probably of the same derivation, although the persistence of the name in Fife, especially in the trade of salt-making which came from Flanders, has given rise to the theory that Younger is from Youncker, a common Flemish name.

But, alas, we do not remain young for ever, and the names Auld and Elder are there to remind us of the fact.

The 100 Commonest Surnames in Scotland

The following table, printed by courtesy of the Registrar General, shows what were the commonest surnames in Scotland in 1976 in descending order of frequency.

What the table does not show is that Smith occurs twice as frequently as Miller (itself a name which has edged up four places in a century). Once one reaches the middle of the list the differentials in frequency are markedly narrower, and at the tail-end there is only a single-figure gap between Mackie (which the Registrar's staff do not recognise as the same name as MacKay) and MacCallum.

Not all the names in the List are Scottish, as witness the Irish imports Kelly, Gallacher, Murphy and Donnelly. Jones, the commonest surname in Wales and the second in England, only just squeezes into our list.

1 Smith	19 Ross	37 Graham
2 Brown	20 MacLean	38 White
3 Thomson	21 Paterson	39 Cameron
4 MacDonald	22 Young	40 Martin
5 Robertson	23 Mitchell	41 Allan
6 Wilson	24 Walker	42 Duncan
7 Campbell	25 Watson	43 Ferguson
8 Stewart	26 Gray	44 Grant
9 Anderson	27 MacLeod	45 Kelly
10 Miller	28 Fraser	46 Black
11 Johnston	29 Henderson	47 Wallace
12 Scott	30 Hamilton	48 Russell
13 Clark	31 Morrison	49 MacGregor
14 Reid	32 Hunter	50 MacMillan
15 Murray	33 Davidson	51 Marshall
16 MacKay	34 Bell	52 Gordon
17 Taylor	35 Simpson	53 Gibson
18 MacKenzie	36 Kerr	54 Wood

55 Gallacher	71 Cunningham	86 Boyle
56 Muir	72 Wright	89 MacLachlan
57 Sinclair	73 Ritchie	88 Bruce
58 Milne	74 Crawford	89 Williamson
59 Kennedy	75 MacIntyre	90 King
60 MacFarlane	76 Douglas	91 Donaldson
61 Craig	77 Docherty	92 Fleming
62 Watt	78 Christie	93 Hill
63 Stevenson	79 Currie	94 Mackie
64 Sutherland	80 Shaw	95 Moore
65 Munro	81 Hughes	96 Finlay
66 Dickson	82 Boyd	97 Murdoch
67 Burns	83 Cook	98 Rae
68 MacIntosh	84 Donnelly	99 MacCallum
69 MacPherson	85 Jamieson	100 Jones
70 Murphy		

Index

68

MacMahon, 43
MacManus, 38
MacMartin, 42
MacMath, 43
MacMichael, 44
MacMichie, 44
MacMillan, **38**, 44, 64
MacMurdo, 45
MacNab, 40
MacNair, 61
MacNicol, 47
MacPartridge, 49
MacPharlane (see MacFarlane)
MacPhee, 39
MacPherson, **39, 40**, 65
MacQueen, 38
MacRae, 40
MacRath, 40
MacRobb, 51
MacRobbie, 49
MacRobert, 51
MacSporran, 40
MacStiofan, 54
MacTaggart, 40
MacTavish, 56
MacThomas, 56
MacVicar, 40
MacWalrick, 27
MacWattie, 49
MacWilliam, 62
Malcolm, 38, 40, **41**
Malise, 41
Manners, 43
Marshall, **41**, 42, 64
Martin, **42,** 64
Massie, Masson, 42
Matheson, **42,** 43
Mathieson, 42
Matthew, Matthewson, 42
Menzies, 43
Michie, 44
Millar, Miller, **43,** 64
Millen, Millin, 44
Millward, 43
Milne, **43,** 65

Milner, 43
Mitchell, **44,** 64
Mollison, 41
Monro, *see* Munro
Moore, 6, 65
Moriarty, 45
Morison, Morrison, **44,** 64
Morris, 44
Muir, 6, 65
Mulcahy, 41
Muldoon, 41
Mulholland, 41
Mullen, 39
Mulligan, 39
Munro, **45,** 65
Murchie, Murchison, 45
Murdoch, 45, 65
Murison, 44
Murphy, 45, 64, 65
Murray, 33, 45, **46,** 64

Napier, 58
Nicol, Nicoll, Nichol, Nicholas, 46
Nicholls, 47
Nicolson, 47
Nixon, 49
Norrie, 53
Novak, 26

Ogg, 63
Ogilvie, 47
Oliphant, 57

Page, 28
Parsons, 40
Pate, 48
Patel, 26
Paterson, Patterson, **48,** 64
Paton, 48
Pattullo, 49
Pitbladdo, 49
Pitcairn, 49
Pitcaithly, 49
Pittendreich, 49
Pope, 28